Masterminding Our Way.
The Power of 5 Minds

Aesha~
I am very happy
our paths have crossed!
Thank you for all you do
to further the field of
social work.

Keep dreaming Big!

Shannon Thomas

OCT 2015

Masterminding Our Way:
The Power of 5 Minds

Create the magic for yourself
and your business!

Sarah Gilliland
Wendy Knutson
Lauren Midgley
Nicole Smith
Shannon Thomas

Copyright © 2015

By Sarah Gilliland, Wendy Knutson, Lauren Midgley,
Nicole Smith and Shannon Thomas.

All rights reserved.

No part of this publication may be reproduced, stored in a retrieval system,
or transmitted in any form or by any means, electronic, mechanical,
photocopying, recording or scanning, or otherwise, except as permitted by
written permission of the Publisher. Requests should be sent
to the Publisher at request@powerof5minds.com.

Limit of Liability/Disclaimer of Warranty: While the publisher
and the authors have used their best efforts in preparing this book,
they make nor representations or warranties with respect to the accuracy
or completeness of the contents of this book and specifically disclaim any
implied warranties of merchantability. The advice and strategies contained
herein may not be suitable for your situation. You should consult with a
professional where appropriate. Neither the publisher nor the authors shall
be liable for any loss of profit or any other commercial damages, including
but not limited to special, incidental, consequential or other damages.

Printed in the United States of America

ISBN : 978-0-9889518-5-3

Published by Focused Action Publishing
Colleyville, TX

I firmly believe you can change your life by what you read, what you listen to, and who your friends are. Change your life by reading Masterminding Our Way, *creating a mastermind group of your friends, and then listening to them!*

> ~ Bob Beaudine, President & CEO of Eastman & Beaudine and best selling author of *The Power of WHO!*

Quick. Think of the toughest challenge you are facing right now. What would it be worth to have a lawyer, CPA, therapist, consultant and sales guru collectively helping you tackle the problem? Unbelievably helpful! Masterminding Our Way *gives you a perspective (from each of the five minds) on how you can build a powerful mastermind that will take your business, and your life, to levels you have always dreamed of.*

> ~ Mike Michalowicz, author of *Profit First*

A true story on how five professional women found a solid way to create a powerful mastermind group to impact their businesses. They share their thoughts on how you can create yours!

> ~ James Malinchak, featured on ABC's Hit TV Show, "Secret Millionaire", author, *Millionaire Success Secrets*, founder, www.MillionaireFreeBook.com

A must read book! Humorous, realistic and powerful. An effective way to get started with the mastermind process!

> ~ Barbara Stanny, author of *Sacred Success* and *Overcoming Underearning*

Your business depends on who you consult with and who you trust. Read this book now to tap into the power of masterminds and fast track your journey to success.

> ~ Linda Swindling, JD, CSP Author of *The Manager's High-Performance Handbook* and *Stop Complainers and Energy Drainers*. CEO of Journey On Training and Development

A great way to maximize your time is to connect with a powerful mastermind group of like-minded individuals. This book will show you how to create one yourself.

> ~ Rory Vaden Co-founder of Southwestern Consulting and New York Times bestselling author of *Take the Stairs*

Your business success depends on who you consult with and who you trust. Clearly, these five women have found the magic of masterminding to impact their business success and personal growth. This book is a must read if you are serious about your growth.

> ~ Judy Hoberman, President of Selling in a Skirt

One of the activities we recommend to all of our coaching clients is to be part of a Mastermind Group. This book will show you how to create one yourself.

> ~ Julie Harris, President and Founder of Harris Real Estate University

Contents

66

In every job that must be done,
there is an element of fun.
You find the fun, and the
job's a game.

99

—P. L. Travers, Mary Poppins

Introduction

Have you ever been sitting somewhere and had a completely unrelated "aha!" moment? That's exactly what happened in May 2014. Our mastermind group had been in full force by this time, and we were each feeling the group's momentum in our individual businesses. Lauren had invited Nicole to James Malinchak's BigMoneySpeaker.com conference.

Lauren became a coaching client of James in the previous year. Nicole felt like a wannabe. Both of them were taking in all the information and strategizing how to incorporate everything they were learning into their businesses. One of the key tools that James and many of his clients use is writing a book. He gave several examples of how he and many others became successful authors. Essentially, they were so passionate about their message that they were able to write best-selling books, delivering their message to many people.

Nicole had a flash of inspiration. She scribbled on her James Malinchak Conference Guide "We should write a book!" Lauren glanced at the notes, knew immediately which "we"

Nicole was referring to, and wholeheartedly agreed.

Nicole and Lauren presented the idea at our next mastermind meeting. After a brief discussion, this book was conceived. True to form for our group, Lauren (our resident published author) took the lead. She called us together for a strategy meeting. We began our journey toward the finished product you're now holding in your hands.

We believe our collective story and our individual stories can serve professionals who, like us, wonder if there is anyone out there who "gets" them. We believe you too, can create your own successful mastermind group.

Our goal is to share who we are, what we do, and how being part of this mastermind group has impacted our businesses and our lives. We'll share step-by-step what to consider should you decide to start your own mastermind. You'll learn how just the mere suggestion of a mastermind group turned us into a synergistic group of businesswomen.

We want you to consider creating your own. It is our goal that we will be successful in inspiring you to do so.

You will meet the five minds who meet with each other regularly. In these pages, you will get to know them, their quirkiness, their strengths, and their passions.

Welcome to our world.

"

You have brains in your head.
You have feet in your shoes.
You can steer yourself any
direction you choose.
You're on your own.
And you know what you know.
And you are the one
who'll decide where to go.

"

—Dr. Seuss, *Oh, the Places You'll Go!*

What Is a Mastermind Group?

In his famous book *Think and Grow Rich*, Napoleon Hill introduces the "Power of the Mastermind." As step nine in his thirteen steps toward riches, Hill describes basically what is known today as a mastermind group. A mastermind group is where synergy is created when several people come together and work toward common goals. Their total mental power is greater than the sum of its parts.

The practice of bringing several minds together to work toward a common goal has been around long before Napoleon Hill. However, he gave it a name: a mastermind group. Since the beginning of mankind, people in a variety of contexts—business, politics, education, religion, military, and the like—have tapped the power of several minds focused on a goal. The simple idea is that two heads are better than one, and if two are better, then three, four, or five heads are even better still.

"

It had long since come to my attention that people of accomplishment rarely sat back and let things happen to them. They went out and happened to things.

"

—Leonardo da Vinci

What Are the Benefits of a Mastermind Group?

Mastermind groups are not for everyone. An effective group should be a case of applying tough love, critical thinking, and creativity. It is not a group of yes-men (or women) placating each other and saying what another wants to hear. Sometimes another person's ideas or thoughts can be hard to hear.

A good mastermind group should challenge each member in an effective way, a way that truly helps that person. Likewise, to be effective, the members must also maintain the utmost respect for one another in offering such challenges and tough love. The words are provided in the spirit that they are there to help one another grow and be successful.

If you're ready to be challenged, then put on your tough skin and get ready to experience the many benefits of a mastermind. Here are just a few of the benefits:

Accountability:

The members of the group can hold each other accountable. Often, verbal commitments are made to each other. Follow-up tasks relative to those commitments are discussed in later meetings.

Beyond the actual accountability, the verbal commitment forces you to think of things for which you want to be accountable. For some, that can be difficult. Sometimes just speaking something out loud can make all the difference. These items of accountability can take the form of goals, plans, or simple next actions.

New/different perspectives:

As we work in our businesses, we're surrounded by people in our own industry, who think like us and often have the same types of ideas and perspectives as we do. By taking our ideas to a group outside of our industry, different perspectives emerge. A unique way of looking at things, "aha" moments, and "Wow! I never thought of it like that" responses are common.

Energy:

Typically, people who are willing to take the time to be in a mastermind group have energy. They are high achievers and see the value of full engagement in a group worthy of their time. But we're not all full of energy all the time. We can feel drained. Coming together in a powerful group can often recharge your battery. The interaction can provide you renewed strength and commitment.

Time to focus outside of the details:

One benefit can be as simple as a forced time to step outside of the details or the day-to-day operations of your business. It is too easy to stay in the weeds, taking care of customers and staff. Stepping back to focus and reflect at a higher altitude is necessary for business growth, business health, and long-term success.

Expand your knowledge and circle of influence:

People in the group bring their knowledge, expertise, experience, and, in a sense, all the people they know. While the group isn't a networking or leads group, it is a place to bring people together and pool resources. Group members don't always do business together and it shouldn't be expected. However, members can be a great resource of people who can benefit each other's expertise and experience.

These five benefits are the standout ones for us. As you create your Mastermind group, you may find other benefits to add to the list.

"

I want to be around people that do things. I don't want to be around people anymore that judge or talk about what people do. I want to be around people who dream and support and do things.

"

—Amy Poehler

Who Are the 5 Minds?

Sarah Gilliland
The Lawyer

Wendy Knutson
The CPA

Lauren Midgley
The Business
Consultant

Nicole Smith
The Realtor

Shannon Thomas
The Therapist

"

Promise me you'll remember you are BRAVER than you believe, STRONGER than you seem, SMARTER than you think.

""

—A. A. Milne, *Winnie the Pooh*

Sarah Gilliland
The Lawyer

Sarah's Favorite Quote—and Why

> *Far better is it to dare mighty things, to win glorious triumphs, even though checkered by failure, than to take up ranks with those poor spirits who neither enjoy much nor suffer much, for they live in that gray twilight that knows neither victory nor defeat.*

> —Theodore Roosevelt

This quote speaks to me because I find myself restless in the "gray twilight" as opposed to those that define it as their contentment. Whether it is in careers, relationships, or pursuing other talents, daring the mighty things, learning from the failures and feeling the glory of the triumphs is really living to me. Failures are still one heck of a ride, and watching something you create blossom and grow is just remarkable.

"

**If you are always trying
to be normal, you will never
know how amazing
you can be**

"

—Maya Angelou

Sarah's Story

Introduction

When first approached to be a part of this mastermind, I couldn't have been more thrilled. I saw the potential for this group in particular to fill a newly present void in my individual professional growth, as well as the trajectory of my business.

I had been invited to join and been a guest of other mastermind groups. I didn't feel that I was a benefit to the group, nor that they were benefiting me, for one reason or another. I have seen from the past experiences and this one that there is a formula for a lasting and beneficial group. The contribution of each member must complement every other member.

Before Business Ownership

I am the co-owner of a law firm and real estate title operation in an affluent area of North Texas. My career since young adulthood has been professionally focused. At eighteen years old, I sent one hundred (very slim) resumes to one hundred attorneys in my college town explaining that I wanted to pursue a law degree.

I indicated that I would appreciate any level of experience

an attorney would be willing to give me. I received two responses. One was a kind lady who explained that she didn't need any staff. The other was the attorney who hired me. After three years, and after excelling in advanced paralegal work, I proceeded to pursue my legal education. Again, in a new town, I continued my legal career while finishing my degree.

Working for small-firm owners for nearly a decade before beginning on my own was more valuable than any class I had taken in my education. I had the privilege of working for some of the best and the worst people as it related to business structure, ethics, people management, money management, and business growth. When deciding to open a firm with my business partners, I was conscientious of a healthy mental list of "dos and don'ts."

In Need of a Mastermind Group

Our business kickoff started better than I could have imagined, due in large part to spending every available hour meeting other local business owners, volunteering, taking leadership roles, and networking in our area. Just shy of a year in business, we experienced the first of many steroid shots our business would enjoy over the years, and I had a 180-degree change in my perspective as a business owner. The fast growth left a need for structure and future planning. Additionally, I was able to see it as a company rather than my baby. We made the decision to hire a business coach team to assist in structuring the growth we desired to see in the future.

Beforehand, I would have been content to own my own job for the rest of my life. My best mentors did so, and I took pride in doing everything related to my skill set of professional services, regardless of how thin I stretched myself.

The coaching opened my eyes to the possibility and desirability of building a company as opposed to building an increasingly demanding job. The changes were big—and painful at times. We made partnership and employee changes. We restructured internal job descriptions. We created a reference manual for all operations within the company. We saw business begin to flood in. We now had the team and operations to handle it. Well.

...coaching opened my eyes to the possibility and desirability of building a company as opposed to building an increasingly demanding job.

If we could do this in only a year, what else could we do?

I was able now to see business and growth through new eyes and to set more ambitious goals. I was eager to seek outside resources and hungry to learn from other experienced business owners how to multiply what we had already achieved. Additionally, I was eager to share my professional epiphany with others.

My business had been involved in networking groups regularly for over a year and realized a huge benefit from it. However, there were also some negative experiences with some networking group structures.

I had been employed by attorneys in the past who partook in paid networking groups. It was robotic and lacked a genuine feel. The members didn't know each other, but they were assigned to the group. Therefore. they were assigned to trusting their client referrals with strangers; referrals garnered you points on a point system.

Other groups required time commitments that were impractical for focusing on business growth, and in others the dedication level of the members was inconsistent.

I was enjoying the concept of groups of professionals helping grow each other's businesses. But at the early stage of my business growth, I was struggling with what was the best fit for me. For my purposes, I ultimately found that genuine, professional, and less structured opportunities to socialize with local professionals lent itself to more solid referral-based growth. Local chambers, community leadership groups, and professional forums provided the relationships with other area business owners that were eager to help each other.

With the networking gap filled and our business coaches' job done, I was in need of a more intimate setting. I wanted to transparently share my day-to-day struggles and triumphs and have safe, honest guidance from an outsider.

Starting the Group

My invitation to join this dynamic group of ladies came

from our revered Wendy. When the email came in, I ran to my partner's office. "I've been invited to join a mastermind group by...(drumroll) Wendy Knutson!" Of course, I would accept. She's a bit of a local professional celebrity.

We giggle a bit now about me perceiving Wendy that way. However, the fact is she is known in our community as a well-networked, well-respected, competent, and professional woman.

For myself, a baby business owner (just about one-and-a-half years at that time) to be viewed by her as a mastermind woman business owner was a humbling compliment and an opportunity I wouldn't pass up. What other business geniuses must she surround herself with?

Forming a new professional group isn't a novel thing. There were dozens of options and opportunities. The proper fit was the only issue for me. I needed full-time professionals, looking to discuss best professional practices (not market to each other), at a schedule I could commit to—people I shared a general commonality with, liked, and trusted.

You *really* have to like and trust these people. When invited to this mastermind, I knew I could check off a couple of my requirements. I was eager to discover if the rest were met. Spoiler alert: They were!

Our initial meeting was a clear-cut "here is what we will be; here is what we won't be" definition of how this group would function. I found that so important and valuable. We were sharing techniques for business growth, ideas and gaining advice from one another.

We were not counting referrals, selling our services to one another, gossiping, or gabbing. We were unveiling the curtains of our businesses for the purpose of full disclosure and honesty among the members. We were absolutely keeping all matters confidential. Each person at the initial meeting was invited to continue or not under the clear understanding and agreement of the structure.

> *We were not counting referrals, selling our services to one another, gossiping, or gabbing.*

All present joined.

Of course life happened as it does, and not all members were able to remain with the group. However, the expectations about structure, respect, and value have been fulfilled without a doubt.

Fears and Fulfillment

As committed as I was, there are always anxieties that accompany a new commitment. I had a faint concern about the group being all women. That was quickly diminished when I met the particular women involved.

My greatest concern with an all-women group was that it would comprise people whose business was last priority in their lives. Would our meetings just be an outlet for drinking and catching up socially? These predispositions came from prior experience, and possibly a bit of stereotype, but were quickly snuffed out.

I had a fear about being the least experienced woman

in the group. I didn't want to hinder the progress of people who had already learned all the business lessons I was just now encountering. I didn't want to be perceived as the taker in the group with nothing to offer anyone else.

Throughout our time together, I've seen the age and time in business to be a minimal factor. All industries have ebbs and flows within them. A new business may have conquered an issue that a veteran has never encountered and vice versa. Veteran business owners may need a fresh view of building new relationships. The new business might need some guidance on established methods from a veteran. Every alternative perspective holds value, which others can learn from if we are open to do so.

I had fears of pressure relating to interconnected industries in the group. Although we are not together to market to each other, we naturally want the others' businesses to do well. To contribute to each other's success, it might mean that we would be adding to each other's clientele.

The questions that went through my mind:
- Would that add an uncomfortable pressure?
- Would I feel reluctant to open up completely around people whom I believe want me as a client?
- Will they show animosity toward me if I don't become a client?
- On the other hand, will I be reluctant to open up to people in the group that fit as my target client?
- Will I make them uncomfortable?
- Might their advice be tailored on an expectation that I

mold my business to be convenient for them individually, but not in a way that is good for my business as a whole?

- Might the group take advantage of our position and expect free or discounted professional services?

These concerns were a bit less answerable by "Yes this happened" or "No it did not". I think the true and honest answer is "Maybe." The solution lies in how the members in the group react to one another and each possible situation. The solution comes back to liking and trusting.

Some degree of interconnection must exist to be a valuable guide to one another. Then when you truly care for one another's business success and each other as people, the feelings of pressure and paranoia are replaced by trust, comradery, and gratitude.

We had the "like," but when does the trust come? The deep trust came slowly and organically. We each had our discussion topics that might have made us a little—or a lot—less comfortable. I believed each of us naturally would receive feedback from the rest that made us want to curse them, then later realize we really wanted to thank them (and only curse them a little, still).

After several months of the same wise women serving as an informal board of directors, the trust began to build up. The gratitude shines through because these women care enough to share a fully honest professional opinion of each of our major business decisions.

The deeper trust also came as we began to allow each

other and ourselves to be people too, not just fellow business owners. I believe the order of things was proper and good. If we had jumped straight into friendships, the kid gloves might have come out instead of the brutally honest voice we sometimes need.

However, if we remained all business for months and years, the connection and trust would be lost. Every meeting has been nearly equally meaningful to me professionally. However, one particular meeting made this group personally meaningful.

A Turning Point

At one significant meeting, I gained a bond with the women of our mastermind greater than the like and trust we had already built.

As a business rapidly grows, you experience bottlenecks in your operations. You just will. The operations on paper are just not as functional as expected, or they aren't properly executed. You muscle through and revamp, but it is a trying time.

For example, if you are an owner of a rapidly growing business, mother of two small boys, wife, pet owner, and a woman who just wants some sleep or to lose twenty pounds.

I haven't had time to come up with an acronym for "her". Some days are a little taste of hell.

One morning, my little taste of hell happened to coincide with our mastermind morning. I was not at my best that day, to say the least. I don't even remember the topic or the question, but we all remember my answer.

Fighting back tears, my answer was "I am just really f^#&ing tired!" I was a bit embarrassed, but I decided it was a "take me or leave me" kind of day. I expected a kind but stern response from the group along the lines of "Sarah, I know we all get there, but let's stay professional and on topic."

But they didn't. In fact, another woman yelled out, "I'm really f^#&ing tired too!" It was an amazing mastermind meeting and day. I very quickly felt energized, refocused, capable, and forever bonded to these amazing women that respect and relate to me.

Point being, the support we give to one another developed beyond our businesses into supporting one another as women business owners. Whether the topic relates to employees, structure, growth, or just being f-ing tired, the mastermind group gives us an outlet to relate and the resource to pull each other and ourselves up by the bootstraps when we need it most.

Going Forward

I am committed to this group and will continue to be as long as we last. Life will happen—and maybe result in some members moving on. We may add more members with the clear standards we have set for ourselves. As time continues, I see ourselves structuring even a bit more.

We now have had the time to understand each of our businesses' milestones and set accountable goals for each other to measure and reach. We like each other, we trust each other—and over our time together, we are incredibly valuable to each other.

Biography of Sarah Gilliland

I am a real estate attorney in North Texas. I am a mother of two boys, married to my college sweetheart and teammate in life. My boys enjoy anything outside, so dirt, bikes, scrapes, and bugs fill our lives with joy.

I grew up in Tulsa, Oklahoma. I had very young, blue-collar parents who split in my early teens. Getting by was the name of the game. Ambition and achievement were luxuries for the middle class. An unfortunate number of my friends did not graduate high school, few went to college, and even fewer finished a degree.

I don't suggest education alone is definitive of a successful future. However, I was surrounded by a culture that highly valued wage working and that defined success by working your way from the warehouse up the ladder.

Entrepreneurs started as rich kids, and you were unquestionably limited to the geographic boundaries of the state of Oklahoma. My grandmother, as an executive director, was the most realistic example of achieving more. I spent most of my final high school years looking to her for guidance on my future.

It was out of a defiant attitude toward the lifestyle I grew up in, and due to the role model of my grandmother, that I moved forward with my education. I met my husband in college, and we chose together to pursue careers and businesses in North Texas.

I gained experience through great mentors but always

had the urge to create and build something of my own. After several years in practice, a series of fortunate and divine-intervention events led to my business partnership.

One of the greatest lessons I've learned as a business owner is that things happen exactly as they should if you let them. Sometimes it is a chance encounter with an old friend, sometimes it is you forcing yourself to go to that meeting you want to cancel, and sometimes it is what falls in your lap. I believe to my core that if anyone can accomplish something, there's no reason that someone wouldn't be me (or you). When you are ready, when you open yourself to it, the best things happen.

"

'Why did you do all this for me?'
he asked. 'I don't deserve it.
I've never done anything for you.'
'You have been my friend,'
replied Charlotte.
'That in itself is a
tremendous thing.'

"

—E. B. White, *Charlotte's Web*

Wendy Knutson
The CPA

Wendy's Favorite Quote—and Why

Just keep swimming

—Dory, *Finding Nemo*

I love this quote because it's to the point and easy to remember. It usually brings a smile to people when they are asked "What is your favorite quote?" When things get tough and I'm not sure of the "next right thing," I remember to "just keep swimming."

"

What if it all goes right?

"

—Mindy Audlin, author of
What If It All Goes Right?

Wendy's Story

My Business

I run a public accounting firm, currently with a staff of ten, including one other CPA. Since seeing my first debit at age seventeen in high school Accounting I, I wanted to be a CPA. Public accounting was always my dream, but I didn't really know what it looked like. Going to school, we CPA students were courted by the big firms (eight at the time). The jobs were rumored to be brutal, including 80–100 hour workweeks.

My dream was to work at a local, public firm. I never saw myself owning my own firm. To be truthful, I just wanted to do accounting. I loved it then and love it now. It just makes sense to me. Even after more than thirty years, I can get giddy over a discussion of tax and accounting. Sometimes, I just want to stand up and shout, "Isn't this amazing?"

I've been asked the question "Am I a successful businesswoman?" I like to think I am, but at the same time it seems like such a foreign concept. I feel passionate about our firm's vision: to enrich the lives of clients and team members by inspiring confidence and delivering meaningful results. I strive to live it daily. If I accomplish this, I would say yes,

I have been successful.

For many years, I struggled with the idea of a work-life balance. I thought this meant having equal time in each. I count things for a living, so working on a schedule and balancing numbers works for me. Recently, however, my focus has become more on health, having a healthy business, healthy marriage, healthy family, and healthy spiritual life.

Owning a business can be all consuming, especially in the start-up phase. It takes a while to find a flow and rhythm, what works and what doesn't. It's trial and error.

The Leadership Journey Begins

From the beginning of my career and into the start of my own business, I participated in networking groups, attended chamber functions, and was involved in community leadership teams. These activities resulted in lots of business-card swapping and glad-handing. Not to mention the time-wasting but "invaluable" one-on-one meetings. I discovered that very few business owners and decision makers attended these groups.

As my business grew, I found myself in more of a leadership role and soon realized that I had a lot to learn. My team was looking to me for guidance and needed me to make decisions. I'm a huge fan of spoken-word entertainment and found my playlist filled with an ever-increasing list of leadership podcasts and audiobooks.

The Desire for a Mastermind Group

I couldn't get enough. There was so much to learn. Repeatedly, I heard of the benefits of joining a mastermind group. Once, I tried to join a mastermind group headed up by a local business coach. The group planned to read several books and walk through the material together. The syllabus also included instruction about and execution of business plans. It was well organized and would be a huge stretch for me professionally, as well as financially.

As a CPA, I tend to gravitate toward things that are organized and well planned. This group looked to be just the ticket for me. The coach had clearly done this before, so I jumped in. However, the group never received enough interest and the project was abandoned. So, I continued devouring leadership audio material as my way of learning and growing.

I asked myself these questions:
- Where were the local business owners?
- Where did they hang out so that I could meet them?
I wondered.

I buried my husband in discussions of the business. It felt as if I was monopolizing all our conversations—not much of a new concept, as I am definitely the more vocal of our team. We began to have little time left to discuss family matters and things that are important to him. But deep down, I wanted our home to be a place separate from the business, an oasis for us.

Another person I trust is my dad. He is a great resource

for me to discuss my business. I regularly consult with him.

But I needed more.

The Need for a Board of Directors

What I needed was an informal board of directors. I needed people who thought like me and wanted the same things from business that I did. A group where I could discuss ideas and get feedback.

When I would encounter people who indicated that they were in a mastermind group, I would eagerly ask about their group. The groups were closed to new members. I was never invited to join. Several people suggested that I start my own group.

Say what? Me?

I'm much too busy. The idea of starting a group was terrifying and overwhelming. I had no idea what was required. Many questions ran through my head.

What was the time commitment? Where would we meet? What format would we use?

How Our Group Started

During this time, my business was in an office complex where we occupied three executive suites. The building contained what seemed to be a greater-than-average number of counselors and business coaches.

We often joked that if a team member was having a bad day or a client was distraught over their tax liability, they could simply walk down the hall for some counseling. I had had some brief chats with one of these counselors, Shannon, several times when our paths had crossed.

On one of these occasions, Shannon mentioned that she was looking for a group as well. I shared my desire of belonging to a group of local business owners, something different from typical networking groups. She seemed interested but wanted a group consisting only of women.

What?

This wasn't what I had in mind. I was concerned that a group of all women would be cliquish and gossipy. I wasn't looking for a social club or coffee klatch. But I had an interested participant; so, I thought, let's see where this goes.

The Invitations Go Out

Later that week, maybe even the same day, Lauren, a friend and fellow Toastmaster, dropped by to bring me a Texas Tech fleece blanket. She knew that my daughter was going to Tech and thought I might like the blanket.

Lauren is a very smart business coach. I like her style. I thought my envisioned group would have a much better chance of success if it included someone with experience and expertise with mastermind groups. Frankly, I was nervous about the preparation and organization time required.

I thought, aha, maybe Lauren would do it. I'm known as a great delegator. So, I asked if she would like to facilitate the mastermind group. She was in, just like that.

In fact, not only would she facilitate, she also wanted

to participate. We started discussing the types of members we wanted, format, and so on right there, that very moment. I told her about Shannon. We agreed that we would start inviting female business owners in the area.

My theory was to over-invite, as you do for a party, thinking that only about half of those invited would join. Boy, was I wrong. At my next Toastmasters meeting I approached Nicole. Nicole was one of the first businesspeople I met when I came to town. She later joined my Toastmasters group, became my niece's realtor, my realtor, and my sister's realtor.

When I approached Nicole, I only got as far as "I'm thinking of forming a mastermind group" when she said, "Yes, yes, yes!" Next, I emailed Sarah, a local, beautiful, poised, sharp-dressing attorney. She was interested too.

The Meet and Greet

Our next step was to schedule a meet and greet. A 7:00 a.m. meeting was my preference, but Shannon couldn't meet until closer to 8:00 a.m. I feared that 8:00 a.m. would interfere too much with my day. I would have to work before the meeting, stop, and go back to work. I felt that if it didn't happen first thing in the morning, it wouldn't happen.

We had several back-and-forth emails. Shannon offered to back out. I was a bit stubborn about it. I just didn't see it working if it wasn't 7:00 a.m. I sat back and waited, not wanting to dictate the situation.

Always the diplomat, Lauren jumped in and offered that we should meet the first time at 8:00 a.m. with everyone. OK, I thought, I'll give it a shot.

I was a bit nervous as I anticipated our upcoming initial meeting. For some, it was their first time to meet. The usual questions ran through my mind. What would the ladies think of each other? Would everyone get along? What would the group dynamic be?

I had brought the group together and knew all but one person prior to the meet and greet. I felt a sense of responsibility for the group. I'm a pretty serious person, especially where my business and money are concerned. Would these ladies be as serious? When I walked in, three of the ladies were already there.

Lauren had notes and an agenda for us. Serious! We started talking about things such as group expectations, plans, and schedules. During that meeting, we planned a "Deep Dive" session where we would have the opportunity to really get to know each other.

I am still amazed that, by the end of the meet and greet, the Deep Dive session was on all our calendars for the next weekend. It was obvious these chicks were serious and they meant business. I started to get

...by the end of the meet and greet, the Deep Dive session was on all our calendars for the next weekend. It was obvious these chicks were serious and they meant business.

the feeling that this would be something special.

This group truly was different. At the very basic level, it was smaller and more intimate than the networking groups I had previously attended. My personality is a much better fit in a small group. When a group gets too large, I tend to shut down. I felt very comfortable with these ladies from the very start.

The Deep Dive

When we arrived at the Deep Dive meeting, all the ladies, seven of us at the time, were prepared. We all were armed with explanations of our business models, brochures, promotional items, and handouts.

I knew this was something special. The commitment for all of us to come together for a half day on a weekend was inspiring. Some of the ladies left behind kids, husbands, and a Dallas Cowboys game (me). These ladies meant business.

The Regular Meetings Begin

After the Deep Dive meeting, we decided we would meet on a twice-a-month schedule for ninety minutes. Our meeting themes have been wide ranging.

In the beginning, the meeting structure was this: Half the members shared their business update for fifteen minutes; the other half gave a five-minute update. Those with the longer time slot brought a question to the group. If possible, the member emailed a question to the group prior to the meeting. Doing so provided the other members time to think and ponder. For the first several months, it was all business.

The Meeting That Changed Things

Then one day, Sarah changed it all. It was Sarah's turn to have a fifteen-minute share. She seemed different. She had no notes, having brought nothing to the meeting. Was she going to share? Did she remember that it was her turn?

She simply said, "I'm so $#$%^ tired." I don't remember the group's reaction, but it was clear that something about that statement changed things. In a way, it broke the ice and took our group to a deeper level.

After that, we were free to share personal as well as business matters. We had become friends as well as mastermind partners. The door was open for the casual random expletive. No walls, no barriers, no pretenses. For me anyway, I was free to be me. This was a safe place.

How This Group Has Affected Me and My Business

Forming friendships has never been easy for me. Generally, I think it's difficult for adults to form friendships. As I raised my kids, I had some "friendships" with women who were my kid's friend's mom. As moms, we spend so much of our time caring for others and not necessarily caring for ourselves.

The women in this group are friends of my choosing. The relationships have been built because of time we choose to spend together. These women care about me. That thought makes my heart swell with joy.

The group has helped me legitimize my business in my own mind by showing me that my business is similar to other businesses I've watched, respected, and seen develop in the community. It has also helped me define the business, answering questions such as "Where do I want to go?" and "Where do I want to be in five years?"

I've never seen myself as having a difficult time with commitment. After all, I've been married for twenty-six years. However, when the group starting asking everyone to share something for which we wanted to be held accountable, I found it to be very difficult. I had to take a hard look at myself and ask "Was I really willing to do this?" People were going to ask me about it later. Crap.

Offering and accepting honest feedback was difficult at first. If I was honest, would they still like me? Would I be able to accept their feedback? I'm very passionate about my business and I tend to get defensive. When folks talk about my business, they're talking about me just the same as if they were talking about one of my kids. It is personal. It's me.

As I watched others in the group give and receive honest feedback, I've learned. I've grown and improved in my ability to give and receive honest feedback inside and outside of the group.

The Board of Directors Becomes a Reality

The reality of this group of ladies becoming my board of directors wasn't clear from the beginning. As we began to trust each other, each displaying her commitment to show up and participate, each showing that we could depend on each other in many ways, the board evolved.

We've Had Our Challenges

The hardest part of the journey, so far, has been losing two members of our original group. One moved out of the area. The other needed to focus on family, rather than business. We discussed how their leaving the group would change our group dynamics. The remaining five are fully committed to our mastermind group.

Why I've Stayed

I've stayed committed because I get so much from the group. Business can be tough. Days can be filled with difficult decisions, scary situations, and uncomfortable confrontations. Sometimes I need a shot of courage, the strength to put on my big-girl panties and show up. I find this strength in the power of the group. Simply imagining Sarah, Shannon, Nicole, or Lauren out there slaying dragons and showing up gives me the courage I need to do the same. We have minimal interaction outside of the meetings, but if I need one of them, all I have to do is send an email, make a call, or text. It's like business 911, like calling Superman or Wonder Woman. They always respond.

Personally and professionally, this year looks to be a very exciting time for me. With our youngest daughter having gotten married recently, our nest is empty. It's as if my husband and I are dating again. For my business, the year is filled with promising changes. We're maturing as an enterprise, honing our craft, finding our core competencies, and serving our niche market.

Biography of Wendy Knutson

Wendy Knutson: wife, mother, business owner, CPA. I am a native Texan, having lived in the Dallas/Fort Worth Metroplex my entire life. I have been married, to Dan Knutson, for more than twenty-six years. We have two daughters, Alicia and Marissa, ages twenty-four and twenty, respectively. In 2014 Marissa married Dylan, blessing us with a wonderful son-in-law. I enjoy spending time with my family, attending church, and participating in church activities. After my faith and family, my passion is business. I find tremendous joy working in my business, both with the team and clients, and in building local relationships. In my spare time, I enjoy knitting.

I graduated summa cum laude with a Bachelor of Science in accounting from the University of Texas at Arlington in 1993. I passed the CPA exam later that year. After a fifteen-year hiatus to stay at home to raise my kids, I began working part-time in my father's business and working as a substitute teacher and elementary school registration clerk. I returned to public accounting in 2006 and received my Texas CPA license in 2008. I served a two-year term as one of fifteen members of Intuit's Accountant and Advisor Customer Council from 2012–2014. In 2015, I became a Certified Profit First Professional.

Knutson CPA, PLLC, in Southlake, Texas, provides accounting and tax services for small-to-medium sized businesses. Our services include various levels of monthly bookkeeping, QuickBooks training and support, and Profit First consulting.

One key differentiator in serving our client is our promise of a twenty-four-hour response time. No more "I can't get in touch with my CPA." We understand that response time is very important to our clients.

Another key differentiator is our up-front, fixed pricing. At Knutson CPA, there are no running meters, no hourly fees, and no surprises. Unlike old-fashioned CPA firms, we don't track time. This allows us to focus on the client and the results they are seeking. We partner with them to build their business. Our vision is to enrich the lives of clients and team members by inspiring confidence and delivering meaningful results.

"

You don't actually do a project;
you can only do action steps
related to it. When enough of the
right action steps have been taken,
some situation will have been
created that matches your initial
picture of the outcome closely
enough that you can call it 'done.'

"

—David Allen, *Getting Things Done: The Art
of Stress-Free Productivity*

Lauren Midgley
The Business Consultant

Lauren's Favorite Quote—and Why

*Finish each day and be done with it. You have done
what you could. Some blunders and absurdities no
doubt crept in; forget them as soon as you can.*

*Tomorrow is a new day; begin it well and serenely
and with too high a spirit to be encumbered
with your old nonsense.*

—Ralph Waldo Emerson

This quote has always had special meaning to me on many
levels.

First, it reminds me that we generally do our best each
day. We need to go to bed feeling good with the results of
our day, rather than thinking we are unaccomplished. No

day is perfect. No human is perfect.

Second, the quote reminds me that the concept of completion feels good. We need to complete tasks, conversations, goals, projects, and other things we have started.

Third, if we are fortunate, we will wake up the next day for another opportunity to live life fully again.

And last, it is unproductive to fret about yesterday and have it affect our "today." Instead, we learn from it and strive to not allow it to affect our spirit.

I live my life looking forward to all the possibilities. Yesterday is done. Ever onward.

“

Amateurs sit and wait for inspiration; the rest of us just get up and go to work.”

”

—Steven King

Lauren's Story

Feeding My Mastermind Soul

I love mastermind groups. Always have. Always will. I was introduced to the concept when I read Napoleon Hill's book *Think and Grow Rich* in the early 90s.

One of the things that stokes my mind the most is the ongoing discussion of an on-point, purposeful topic with others who are intelligent and willing to share their point of view. My favorite topic is how to grow a business. My favorite audience is forward-thinking business owners seeking to build a legacy.

As an admitted workaholic, I love the business of business. I revel in hearing about others' businesses, such as the following.

- How they got started
- What their passion for starting the business was
- Their why, so I can understand them better
- Their current struggles and how they are overcoming them
- What they are doing to grow their business
- What they are doing to grow themselves as leaders
- The best practices they are willing to share with others

Mastermind sessions with other trusted souls feed my admitted brainiac mind and soul. Currently, I am involved in two masterminds, one that is very industry specific to my profession of public speaking and this one that is made up of people in a variety of industries.

So when Wendy Knutson, a successful and professional CPA I knew from my Toastmaster club, suggested the concept of a local mastermind, I knew that I was definitely interested in being a part of that group. Wendy is well connected. She felt that now was the time to make this happen.

My Background on Masterminds

I have been part of two other masterminds. In 2011, I had just recently started my consulting business. During that time, I was highly active in local networking to meet other business owners and potential prospects. The concept of masterminds seemed to be a common topic. Another lady and I were the co-leaders of our newly created mastermind of a group of six local businesswomen interested in growing their businesses, which covered a variety of industries.

Immediately, one lady decided that she would not have the time or desire to make the full commitment to the group due to family happenings. I was grateful that she figured that out early on, rather than provide a half-hearted attempt. Approximately six months later, another lady moved from the area, making it difficult for her to continue meeting with us. The power in our meetings was getting together in person, not virtually.

So we were down to four people. One thing I learned about this process is that you do need enough people to have the right energy, mind power, wisdom, and sharing of experiences. This group of four lasted another four months until there was mutual agreement to disband this mastermind. The positive outcome for me was that I remain friends with the other three women. We still fully support each other's mission and business.

Masterminding in a Corporate Setting

The other mastermind that I participated in was in 2007, when I worked at a corporate headquarters of a franchise company. I was invited to join an elite, successful group of eight franchisees who represented our company products in the marketplace. They had assembled a mastermind group. I felt honored to be part of the group as a facilitator to represent the company's point of view.

This group met via phone and twice a year in person. This group lasted approximately two years, with an incredible amount of progress and growth in all the businesses. The interesting side benefit was watching these eight individuals grow as individuals and leaders.

When a mastermind group begins to form, I find that there is a curiosity about who is going to join, how well you think you know them, who is going to commit to the concept of sharing information, what their challenges are, and whether their chal-

When a mastermind group begins to form, I find that there is a curiosity about who is going to join...

lenges are similar to yours or much different. Your initial thoughts are all about how this group will be successful.

These two very different experiences provided insight on:
- how and why masterminds work
- the lifecycle and longevity of them
- how personalities can impact the group both positively and negatively
- the progress a business owner can make by being associated with a mastermind group.

Key Lessons I Learned from My Earlier Experiences

Participants have to be ready in their heart and mind to commit to the concept of the mastermind. They must be willing to be open-minded to others' points of view. A key factor is to realize that different personality types see the world differently, and that it is okay to not be "right" all the time.

Advance preparation for the meeting makes a huge difference as to what can actually be accomplished at the meeting, whether face-to-face or over the phone.

Even though we started out as merely business associates, I found that the more I learned about them personally—how they thought about their businesses and their lives—I found that I fell in love with each of them as a person.

I thoroughly enjoy seeing personal development in others. This is just another one of my quirky geek characteristics. So I loved seeing the growth in others and pointing out their progress to them. In this process I observed, those who were all in and willing to have open minds made incredible personal and business progress.

The mastermind process does have a lifecycle. Some in the group will leave due to life situations that arise. That is okay. But when change happens it does impact the dynamics of the group. Most groups will readjust to the new makeup of the smaller group. New members added to the existing group will also change the dynamics, and hopefully in a positive way.

Masterminding with an All-Women Group

What led me to think that a mastermind was the right thing for my business at this time was threefold:

1. I missed being part of a mastermind group; it had been at least eighteen months since I was involved with one. As I mentioned earlier, I crave that type of brainiac interaction.

2. I was in the midst of a shift in my business model from consulting as my lead revenue generator to professional speaking. Thus, I wanted to associate with others who could provide perspective on my business ideas.

3. I was ready to, with those I trust, hear the honest truth to provide validation and critical review of my ideas. I was ready to receive challenges when needed. And most important, I was ready to have accountability partners help me honor my stated commitments. I needed them to hold my feet to the fire on what I wanted so desperately to accomplish.

Setting the Right Expectations Will Lead to Success

Expectations that I had for myself in the beginning were the usual ones for me:

1. Build a relationship with everyone in the group
2. Understand their business model and industry
3. Commit to be present at every meeting to listen to their words and needs
4. Seek my own clarity and ask for what I needed from them
5. Share my talents as a business consultant
6. Speak up and not hold back, but respecting their dignity

Expectations that I had for the others in the beginning:

1. Commit to attend each meeting
2. Start on time, end on time
3. Come prepared to discuss your business
4. Stay focused on the business topics planned for our meeting
5. Be honest at all times
6. Understand that we do not have to do business with each other
7. Be present at the meeting; not on the phone or email

As with any new group, you may not know everyone in the group. In my case, I knew three ladies. Two were from my Toastmaster group, and one lady I recruited to join us, based on her energy and commitment to her personal development and success.

For the other three that I did not know, I knew that it was up to me to make sure that I learned more about them: what is important to them, what they are motivated by, their family life, and their passions outside of their businesses. By knowing these other aspects, you build the likeability and trust factors.

How We Got Started

Wendy was the catalyst of the idea to make this mastermind group happen. She approached me after a Toastmaster meeting. I loved the idea.

Initially, we had a meet and greet at a local coffeehouse where we could talk about ourselves, our businesses, and what we were looking for in a mastermind group.

Each person was referred in by someone else.

My initial impression of this group of women was WOW!

A variety of ages, backgrounds, educational levels, and industries. An important factor was that all were very active in their business, significant breadwinners in their family, and interested in personal development and growth.

We all had been in business for at least three years, had customers, had cash flow, and had a huge desire to take our businesses to the next level.

As you can imagine, this was music to my geeky ears. Wendy had asked me to be the facilitator of the group. I was very excited, as I enjoy that role. So I thought, if I am going to do a great job as a facilitator, I want to work with a committed group.

Initially, we started with seven of us. The profile of the group:

- Variety of ages: 28–56
- Smart, intelligent businesswomen

- Successful in our respective businesses and know how to make money
- Diverse industries (CPA, real estate, business consultant, executive director of a nonprofit, psychotherapist, insurance agent, attorney)
- Forward, positive thinkers
- Beyond the start-up mode in our businesses
- No one personality dominating the group
- All were committed to showing up and being present at the meeting
- All meetings done face-to-face
- Incredible respect for each other
- Willing to speak the truth to each other in a kind, dignified way

The Types of Topics We Discuss

- Our biggest business challenge facing us right then
- Goals for upcoming time frame
- The one thing that will move our business's "growth needle"
- Marketing ideas

Why I Enjoy This Group

I look forward to our twice-per-month meetings. One of my key beliefs is that our businesses do change over time based on changed strategies, new marketplace needs, and new opportunities. The main mission of the business may be the same, but strategies and action plans evolve. Since we meet frequently, we are able to stay connected with the changes that happen in each of our businesses and in our lives.

As would be expected, we did have changes with our group. Within nine months of the inception, one of our members moved to Chicago during the summer. She would call into our meetings virtually. By the end of the summer, she made the decision to make a permanent move to Montana.

We as a group supported her decision, pointed out pros and cons, and reassured her that we were just a phone call or email away. All of us believed it was in the best interest of the group that we not try to force her participation via phone at our meetings. The magic of the meetings is the face-to-face interaction and energy.

Another change happened shortly thereafter when another member had a significant event happen in her personal life that forced some necessary decisions about her business and family. She decided that continuing with the group was not in her best interest at that time.

A flashback to the beginning with all seven of us meeting as a potential mastermind group.

Our initial meeting began at the coffee shop. The next meeting was at my house; it lasted three hours. I wanted it to be casual so that we could openly and confidentially speak about ourselves, our businesses, our hopes, and our dreams. We did exactly that.

We set the dates for our schedule of upcoming meetings. We stated our commitment to attend and be prepared for each meeting. Luckily, Wendy and Shannon had an office space where we could use the conference room. It was very important that our meeting space had a closed door, so that we could speak freely and confidentially.

I knew by the first two meetings that we had the right group in place. All were willing to follow the guidelines for a solid, on-point meeting. Everyone showed up on time.

As the facilitator, I love this group. Why?

- They are willing for me to be the timekeeper to keep them on track and allow time for all to speak.
- They are open to my comments that we were getting off topic and are open to being reined back in, when needed.
- They are listening intently to what the presenter is saying and are providing honest feedback.
- They are showing their humanness and vulnerability about what personal factors impact the running of a business.

We saw tears. We felt the raw human emotion. We shared funny stories. We shared sad stories. We hugged each other before and after the meeting. We used "bad" words. We used "good" words. We used made-up words. We created inside jokes. We made up secret acronyms that only our group knows the true meaning of.

Most important of all, we began to know each other on such a deep level. There was one standout meeting that started us down the path of no return. It was early in our journey with one another … maybe the third or fourth meeting.

One of us, Sarah, broke away from the strictly business format. During that meeting, she wanted to talk about where she was personally, not about the business.

Immediately we all saw that she was quite upset. The hurt she felt was quite visible. As she described her situation, I noticed the other heads in the room nodding up and down. We related so much to her words and situation. We felt empathy. We were in her shoes.

That meeting broke the ice.

From that meeting on, we knew that it was okay to share what was happening to us personally as a backdrop to how it impacted our business. As each meeting unfolded, each of us felt that it was okay to share more bits and pieces of the person we really are.

Within those sanctified walls, we learned about each other. We deepened our caring for one another. We supported each other during and outside of the meeting.

At no time have I ever felt that there was gossiping going on about each other or ugly intent. We are fortunate in that we, over time, became real and authentic with each other as each of the sessions continued to roll out.

I know that the information we discuss is kept strictly confidential. We did not sign a confidentiality agreement, but it was understood from the beginning that confidentiality was necessary in order to build trust with each other. My belief is that we have held to that standard.

How the Mastermind Has Impacted My Business

This group has impacted me and my business in many ways. It forces me, as the facilitator, to think about what topics our group should discuss about our businesses at the next meeting. Oftentimes, it is a continued conversation on a topic we partially covered at the last meeting.

I listen and learn about their businesses. That information helps me immensely when I am working with my consulting clients. If these mastermind ladies are having issues in their business, then it is highly likely that my clients might be experiencing similar situations.

This group is like a laboratory for me to learn more about the "business of business" ...

This group is like a laboratory for me to learn more about the "business of business" shared by them in a real, authentic way.

At one of the meetings, we had a male (gasp!) guest who provided us insight into our personalities and how we use our natural personalities in running our businesses. I loved this information because it provided huge insight about and validation of my personality. But it also provided insight into my compadres' personalities.

Using this information, we were better able to understand how we used our natural wiring as we approach our business, our logic, our emotions to impact results. My huge "aha" moment was the horizontal scale that showed how emotional or stoic a person could be. My score was a 10 on stoic.

That score explained a lot for me about why my approach to many aspects in my life and business is NOT to show emotion.

Why I Stay Committed to This Group

The main reason I stay committed is that I truly enjoy each of these ladies. They are rock stars in their professions. They are fun. They are real. I trust them implicitly. I know they have my best interests at heart, as I do for them.

I want to see them succeed and capture their dreams. I applaud all their efforts and learning as we move through this journey together.

I know that each meeting will bring new information for each of us. The clarity gained through our discussions is nothing short of amazing. We listen to each other's viewpoints knowing they are offered with wisdom and caring.

One of the other key reasons I stay committed is that we share knowledge about resources in the marketplace. I trust their opinions. If they say I should consider person X as a resource to accomplish a task, then I trust their judgment.

If one person in the group recommends a book or a podcast on a specific topic, we all trust that person's opinion and obtain that information.

I am committed to the three hours a month to continue these valuable relationships. The payoff is huge.

How Will This Group Impact Me in the Future?

These ladies are my trusted resource for holding me accountable and keeping me on track in my business. I admire their forward movement in their business. They inspire me to stay actionable.

I am cautious about whom I open up to, given my stoic

nature. I think about three questions as I approach business relationships:

1. Does this person strive for excellence?
2. Does this person care about me?
3. Can I trust this person?

If any of those unspoken questions are answered with a no, then I know that I am naturally guarded with the amount of information I will share.

With this group of ladies, the answer to those questions for me is a resounding YES!

Biography of Lauren Midgley

I am a business consultant, professional speaker, and author who has lived in the Dallas/Fort Worth area for the past eleven years. Six states have been my home: Ohio, Arizona, California, Pennsylvania, Maryland, and Texas. Divorced after fifteen years of marriage, I am back to being single (for nine years as of this writing) and in a committed relationship. My children are young adults, ages seventeen and twenty. With one in college, and one soon to head to college, I look forward to having a living environment where it is just me, the two cats (my daughter's), and the significant other.

As a brainiac, I have always loved learning and still do. I finished high school in three-and-a-half years; I was getting antsy to get on with life. Following the same pattern, I finished my undergrad degree in three-and-a-half years at Arizona State University, majoring in marketing and minoring in finance. An overachiever, I graduated with the distinction of magna cum laude. All that means is that my grade point was above 3.75. I felt very accomplished about that, because I worked full-time through college to pay for my schooling and living expenses.

After being in the work world for five years, I decided it was time to go back to school to obtain the coveted masters degree in business administration (MBA) from Golden Gate University in San Francisco, California. My thinking at the time was that since my company was willing to pay for my education, then I should invest the time. Two years later, after completing ten courses, I had my coveted MBA.

With the MBA in hand, I convinced the senior director of marketing of my company that he "needed" my expertise (at the young age of twenty-nine) in his marketing department. Thus, I was promoted to director of a specific product at our company's headquarters in Pennsylvania. So I made the move from the West Coast to the East Coast.

Overall, my career consisted of working for two Fortune 500 companies in sales, sales management, and marketing roles. The company that paid for my MBA was the one where I experienced the most growth personally and professionally in the seventeen years I was employed by them. Twelve of those years I was in a vice-presidential role.

Furthering my education, I sought many professional development courses from Dale Carnegie, to Miller Heiman Strategic Selling, to Influence Management, to becoming a Certified Franchise Executive (CFE) through the International Franchise Association.

Eventually, my time in corporate world needed to come to an end. It was my choice to leave the lucrative six-figure-income vice-president position. I was chomping at the bit to do more, be more, and impact more. Thus, in July 2010, I started my own company, Courage to Succeed Consulting.

As a lifelong learner, I continued to seek out professional development avenues. I rejoined Toastmasters for two reasons: 1) maintain my presentation skills and 2) network with other professionals. Less than two years later, I earned the Distinguished Toastmaster (DTM) certification, which less than 1% of all Toastmasters achieve.

I was fascinated with the concept of public speaking, loved meeting professional speakers, and knew I wanted to be one of them. In 2012, I joined the local Texas chapter of National Speakers Association to further my professional development and hang with my tribe. Two years later, I was asked to be on the board of directors for the local chapter. My business today consists of consulting with companies on their business growth strategies, leadership, and productivity. I utilize speaking as a business strategy to communicate my message and to attract consulting engagements. The focus of my work with others is on productivity, how that will impact the profits of their businesses and quality of their lives.

I have written a book that I call my "starter book." Early on as I was embarking on the speaking path, many others told me I needed to have a book. At that time, I was coaching and doing workshops on the topic of procrastination. I believed (and still do) that we as a society have allowed this bad habit to impact our lives. Helping others overcome this habit became a passion of mine.

I wanted to learn how to publish this book. So being the learner type, I found a local coach and author, Michelle

Prince, who guided me through the steps of independent publishing. I am forever grateful to her for her wisdom and willingness to share the publishing process.

I have two other books that I intend to publish in 2015.

"

Seek first to understand, then to be understood.

"

—Stephen R. Covey, author, habit 5 of
The 7 Habits of Highly Effective People

Nicole Smith
The Realtor

Nicole's Favorite Quote—and Why

> *Success is never owned. It is only rented.*
> *And the rent is due every day.*
>
> —Rory Vaden in *Take the Stairs*

I love this quote because it reminds me that we are called to do and be the best we can every single moment of every single day. For those of us who value success, this inspires us to remember that success isn't a given. The work we did to get us the success we wanted may be different than the work we do to keep us successful, but the work never stops. Success is definitely not something to take for granted.

"

Do not let the behavior of others destroy your inner peace.

"

—the Dalai Lama

Nicole's Story

I'm one of those who rereads Napoleon Hill's *Think and Grow Rich* annually; and that's where I learned about the "mastermind" concept. Over the years, I have wanted to be part of a mastermind group, but I had never taken the time to create one myself and had not been asked to join one.

Once I found out about the opportunity to be a part of this mastermind group, I knew that I wanted and needed it for this season of my business life. I was open to the idea that this one may or may not be a match for me and my goals, but I had decided that if it wasn't, it would be the right time to create one. I was honored to have been asked by Wendy to participate, and once I met the other professional women involved, I knew I wanted to be a part of this mastermind group.

As a residential real estate agent, I have helped hundreds of families buy and sell homes in the Dallas/Fort Worth area for the past twenty years. "Success" is a broad word. I am a member of the RE/MAX Hall of Fame and hold numerous designations awarded on the basis of sales production and education, and I have been recognized by *Texas Monthly, D Magazine, Dallas Business Journal, Fort*

Worth Business Press, and *Fort Worth, Texas Magazine* as a top realtor.

However…

The biggest determiner of my feeling successful is that 90% of my business each year is repeat clients and referrals. Knowing that my clients value me and my service enough to refer me to their friends, families, and associates is the best "award" I could ever receive. And, as much as I have enabled my business to define my "success," my greatest source of pride is my children.

I grew up in a small Texas town with small Texas ideas—lots of lack and limitation in my genetics. As a senior in high school in 1984–85, I was national vice-president of Future Business Leaders of America and was given the opportunity to travel the country and speak to (and with) entrepreneurial-minded high school students and leaders. That didn't seem to impact me much as I chose to attend a very small college close to home and marry my college sweetheart at twenty-one.

A few years later, after leaving a comfy pharmaceutical sales career to venture off into the "risky" world of residential real estate, I was introduced to the works of Jim Rohn, Tony Robbins, Brian Tracy. My world has never been the same.

Since that time, I have been actively on the journey of self-development and exploring the limitless opportunities for prosperity and contribution to this big world.

Life hasn't always been easy—divorce, a house

destroyed by fire, financial devastation when the real estate market turned, challenges (and joys) of single parenting—but it has always been meaningful, and I am grateful to have had each and every experience that has made me who I am today.

Business Development

As a realtor, I have done anything and everything to generate business. Some of my not-so-proud moments include stuffing a *Homes Magazine* with information about me and my services. I didn't realize that the owner of the magazine would have an issue with that! Also, I put a business card with a "Call Me & I Will Help with Your Relocation Process" sticker under the windshield wiper of every car in a local hotel parking lot. I've done every single other possible lead-generation technique over the years.

My focus for the ten years prior to this mastermind group was business-to-business networking. If there was a networking group to join and attend, I was there. My primary focus was my local chamber of commerce, where I led a networking group, served as an ambassador, chaired the Ambassador Committee, and served a three-year term on the board of directors. I spent a tremendous amount of time and energy creating relationships and giving back to my community through this organization. I also was part of a BNI networking group for several years but ultimately found its value to be far less than the amount of time and money I was investing.

I have advertised, done direct mail and online advertising—you name it, I've probably done it. I had not ever done a mastermind group before, so when the opportunity presented itself, I jumped on it. Since becoming part of this group, I have stopped attending networking group meetings though I still believe in the concept. I just found that there were better uses of my time than bebopping around to meetings all the time.

Though I was worn out from traditional networking, I knew I needed to continue a connection with other business owners—not necessarily to generate more business, though that was certainly something I was open to, but mainly to connect with fellow business owners. I am a learner—always seeking new information, ideas, and connections—and I thought this would be a way to connect deeply with a small group (vs shallowly with a larger group).

Mastermind vs. Networking

In the beginning, I wasn't sure what I expected. I thought that, at worst, it could be a huge waste of time and energy (but that didn't scare me, because I've wasted plenty of time and energy on other business-building ideas). At best, I thought it would be an educational environment where I could expand and grow my business through the relationships I would be creating.

Having been in many networking groups that had attendance requirements in order to keep your spot in the group, I knew the value of regular attendance. Communicating it to the group set the stage for all of us to be held accountable to the same standards. I knew that I didn't want to miss anything—too much can happen between meetings, and if there was a "oh—you had to be there" moment in a meeting, and individuals weren't there, it would foster disconnection.

Not only did the commitment and attendance expectations make sense to me, I believe they are part of the foundation that makes a group work. In fact, we learned this with an original member who relocated. As much as I appreciated her contribution to the group, having her on speakerphone was just not the same as having her in the room.

It was clearly conveyed in the beginning that this group would (potentially) become our personal board of directors. Though the idea appealed to me, it was also a little foreign to me since I didn't know several of these ladies at all prior to our first meeting. I was curious to see how the transformation from being strangers to trusted advisors would occur... If it would occur.

Given my exhaustion with traditional networking groups (gabfests), I decided that if this group activity became just a lot of talking, I would not want to continue my involvement. I knew it just wouldn't be productive.

Fortunately, getting into that zone is the exception and not the rule, and when we sometimes slide down the slippery slope that is chattiness, that zone has proven to be instrumental in deepening our relationships with one another.

I didn't really slow down long enough in the beginning to really specify my fears—perhaps I should have. In looking back, however, one of my primary concerns was whether or not this would be a meaningful use of my time. I work many hours, so the idea of having to "give up" three hours each month for another meeting was a big concern to me initially.

It was important to me that we not automatically be "required" (or feel obligated) to do business with the other group members—though now that I have a relationship with everyone, I can't imagine NOT doing business with the others. The key is not requiring it (as they do in many true networking groups).

And, in hindsight, I was concerned that I might not really like some of the ladies, and that if I didn't, fulfilling the initial commitment might be a challenge. But, given that our initial commitment was relatively short (six months), I opened myself to the possibility of not liking all of them (I knew I liked two of the other six) and being willing to fulfill the minimum commitment regardless.

Getting Started

The meet and greet was critical for my commitment level. I already knew two of the original six ladies, so I was pretty much in. The initial meeting was instrumental in assuring me that these were "nice" women, and women I could learn something from. Based on that meeting, I was sold on the idea of committing to the initial six-month term.

The second meeting was the all-afternoon one at Lauren's house. It was a little long and, though necessary, felt more like a "resume delivery" time. It seemed like everyone was trying to tell their whole life story in twenty minutes or less.

However, I knew this mastermind was meaningful right off the bat.

Once I heard everyone's story and had the opportunity to share mine, I knew we had the opportunity to make some magic happen.

Once I heard everyone's story and had the opportunity to share mine, I knew we had the opportunity to make some magic happen.

I leave every single meeting without exception with a new book (or two or three) to pick up and read, a new podcast to tune in to, a new perspective on my business and life, and an action item for immediate implementation.

The Shift—Getting Real

The most memorable meeting for me, early on, was when Sarah admitted to being "f-ing tired." I could SO relate to that. I think that was the beginning of everyone being REAL. From then on, even though we talked about our businesses, there was a personal side, too.

And, in addition to being successful businesspeople— we acknowledged the similar challenges of being successful businesswomen. And how much pressure is on us to maintain our homes, our families, our relationships, our futures, AND our businesses.

Another real moment of connection occurred for me once we did the personality analysis Culture Index. Some of the members in the group have an extreme red dot (reflecting strong, dominate leadership tendencies). Each of us thinks we need to pull that dominance back in order to be successful. Acknowledging that a room full of men with extreme red dots would likely not have the same belief of the need to contain or disguise the level of dominance was very illuminating and connecting.

Impact on My Life and My Business

This group has positively impacted my business on many levels. On the surface, my marketing pieces have been critiqued and changed; my hiring (or not-to-hire) decisions have been challenged and affirmed; and my target audience has shifted—all as a result of comments made during meetings.

There have been several times when I held back my opinions and feedback, but primarily due to time constraints. For the most part, I am very willing to provide honest feedback—sandwiching the "negatives" between two "positives." I am committed to being honest because I want and need honesty from the other members. It was hard, at first, to give some less-than-positive feedback, but the recipient appreciated the honesty.

I trust these ladies and their opinions.

More impactful, however, is what is below the surface. What no one would know if I didn't disclose it: Being part of this group has expanded my perspective. My business can be like working in a tunnel with only realtors on either side. In the past, I made many decisions based on what I see in my industry only. It has been refreshing (and exciting) to have the perspective of professional women in other industries on my specific business.

I am a better person today because of the books, podcasts, and events that are recommended by the ladies in this group.

Accountability is something we touch on from time to time, but overall, that has not been the focus. We leave this up to each individual. Currently, I'm an accountability partner for one of our members, but it is because she specifically asked to be held accountable.

Typically, having a theme to our meeting helps keep us focused on the business at hand—kind of like guardrails. Even so, I have always felt safe to go outside the theme if my business needed some immediate input from the group. Even when I used my time to discuss something other than the theme, having the theme in advance stretched me to really evaluate areas of my business and life that needed to be explored—regardless of whether or not I discussed the details with the group. Having an effective facilitator (thank you, Lauren!) is critical for this to work.

Staying committed to this group has been surprisingly easy.

I realized how impactful this small group is, in comparison to the bebopping around I had been doing for the past ten years. I exhaled and dove in.

If I were still doing all those other activities, the time commitment to this group would have been a stretch. But because the majority of those prior activities were optional and not nearly as impactful, I chose this group. I've grown to love each member, their personality and perspective they each bring to our group. I feel connected to a positive outcome for us all.

What's Next

> *There are always variables beyond my control, but I can control my attitude, my activities, and my associates.*

It's difficult to project what the next year will look like in my business. There are always variables beyond my control, but I can control my attitude, my activities, and my associates. I will choose to be positive, generous, and competent; to focus on productive business-generation and management activities; and to associate with like-minded businesswomen in my mastermind group.

Biography of Nicole Smith

A **fifth-generation** Texan, I strive to embody a down-to-earth, no-nonsense approach to life and business. A licensed real estate agent since 1995, I have had the pleasure of helping hundreds of families move to, from, and around the Dallas/Fort Worth area.

To illustrate my commitment to provide the most competent possible service to my clients, I have earned industry designations including Certified Residential Specialist, Accredited Buyer Representative, Luxury Home Marketing Specialist, Real Estate Divorce Specialist, and Senior Real Estate Specialist.

In addition to being consistently recognized as a leader in the real estate industry in such publications as *D Magazine*, *Texas Monthly*, *Fort Worth Business Press*, and *Dallas Business Journal*, I am especially proud of being a Miracle Agent, with a portion of each closing being contributed to Children's Miracle Network in my client's honor.

Fundamentally, I believe that our homes create the chapters in the story of our lives. My real estate business is founded on my commitment to improve the lives of those I serve by taking care of my clients before, during, and after a transaction.

I have been referred to as a "creative marketer", "accomplished strategist", and "proven negotiator" of residential real estate. My business continues to grow thanks to referrals and repeat business from my many wonderful clients.

I am the proud mother of two grown children—my greatest achievement to date. Toastmasters, numerous community organizations and events receive my attention when I'm not helping families buy or sell a home. I love to travel. I find humor in documenting the many lessons I learn about life from my dog, Honey.

"

It's no use to go back to yesterday because I was a different person then."

"

—Lewis Carroll, *Alice's Adventures in Wonderland*

Shannon Thomas
The Therapist

Shannon's Favorite Quote—and Why

*Being an entrepreneur is definitely not the safe road.
But that's also the fun and adventure of it.*

—Alexandra Kenin

I chose this quote as my favorite because it strips down everything that is important to me. A good quote just vibrates positive things in our hearts and spirits when we see it and this quote does exactly that for me.

The word "entrepreneur" jumps out. As a counselor in a private practice, a lot of professionals in my industry don't see themselves as an entrepreneur. I absolutely 100% identify with that description. In order to enjoy any measure of success as a small-business owner, we must have an entrepreneurial mind-set, drive, and unwavering level of commitment to see our business succeed.

Entrepreneurs know how to get things done. They know how to think outside of the standard business-life box and how to get excited, rather than bogged down, by the pressures that come when it all rides on you and you alone.

Not the safe road. That sentence can be really scary—stepping out of our comfort zone and into a lane for which there are no maps can be overwhelming. It is also exactly where really wonderful personal growth happens, and fun and adventures that could not have been dreamt are possible.

The road of being an entrepreneur doesn't have to be full of pitfalls and cliffs. It can be amazing. It can be successful. I think that's why this quote is my favorite one. It reminds me that I am in fact a woman who has chosen to not rely on someone else for a paycheck. It is a fabulous journey along the way.

"

The future won't take care of itself; I must take care of it

"

—William Petersen

Shannon's Story

What Didn't Work

Honestly, I am not sure I was entirely attracted to the concept of being a part of a mastermind group. I am an introvert and my fill of people is met remarkably quickly. The idea of being expected to meet with the same group on some sort of regular schedule and format worried me. The concept kind of cramped my social style.

With that said, I had been looking for something that would help serve as an education platform and maybe get me in contact with other business owners. I felt isolated within my business and especially among women in my community. I live and own my business in the proverbial burbs. I felt surrounded by primarily stay-at-home moms. Many of them homeschooled their children so the women weren't even available during the day.

With my industry being private practice counseling, I felt even more isolated because I had no one as a true co-worker. I am the sole agency owner. Having staff members is very different than having business peers with whom I can come off the stage and be vulnerable about my own business struggles and achievements. The isolation I was feeling at the time drove me to want to find an outlet to fill the professional void.

When I began thinking about finding a business-owners group, I had hoped it would be a limited time commitment but maybe provide workshops on running a small business, advertising, or finances. It was my desire to informally meet a small-to-medium-sized group of people (workshop-type setting) and maybe foster closer connections with one or two other participants.

One area of my counseling specialty is executive coaching. Several of my clients had shared that they were or had previously been in professional peer groups that functioned as a close-knit circle of confidantes; made up of other C-Level folks (CEO, CFO and the like). My personality is such that I keep my friendship group very small. I didn't want big emotional commitments to a whole new group of professionals. However, I secretly loved the idea of being encouraged by and learning from other business owners.

I had heard of an organization that had different local groups that met and provided all-day seminars and other smaller get-togethers. The format was first a luncheon to visit with other people who were already in a cluster group and to meet newcomers, like myself.

I contacted the local representative for the branch and got my name on the list for the next meeting. On the day of the luncheon, I wasn't thrilled about going as it felt like just another thing on my to-do list.

However, I convinced myself that they were meeting at a nice country club close to my office and I might meet some friendly people. I figured the lunch would probably be good. Even though I wasn't sure of what to expect, I knew that something internal was driving me to pursue it further. I wanted something to add to my business but I just hadn't yet figured out what it was or how I was going to find it.

I attended the newcomers' meeting and it had some really great aspects to it. The education piece I was looking for would definitely have been found within this organization. The group was mixed, men and women, with the vast majority being men. All the participants had been doing business for some time. Each had achieved a baseline level of success. I knew I would be able to learn things from the people in the group and that appealed to me.

However, at my core being, I was turned off by the tone and basic nature of that particular organization. For some people it would work but for me this group was much too religious and overt in their beliefs.

I know that is ironic for the one of the five mastermind members who has "Christian" in her business title to say that another group was too churchy. But they were and it turned me off.

I wasn't looking for a sermon about owning a business. I was looking for people to do business life with and to learn from along the way.

Another caveat of the group was all the testosterone. It

was thick in the room! I think of the twenty people present, there were three women, including myself. A major turnoff is when businesswomen feel the need to morph their femininity toward a masculine stance. I could see that dynamic easily happening within the group.

Given that it was a religious business-owners group full of men, there was a patriarchal undercurrent toward the three women in the room. As you can imagine, that style didn't sit too well with me. I wasn't in need of a group of men who maybe felt it was their role to shepherd me and watch over me as one of the little women of the group. That attitude was not going to fly with me at all.

The final piece that sealed my no-go on pursuing the group was the financial commitment. Yikes. By my standards it was really expensive. I felt like a child with a lemonade stand next to the other very wealthy businessmen in the room. I am perfectly fine with being a small fish in a big pond but I couldn't even afford to get into this particular pond.

With the realization that this group was not going to meet my needs, I finished my lovely country club shrimp salad, said the usual pleasantries that I would be thinking about whether to join the group, and left.

I was fairly disappointed as I drove back to my office. I was looking for something that was missing in my business life. Yet again, I had not found it. I didn't fit in with the stay-at-home mom crowd and now, I didn't fit in with the wealthy businessmen crew.

I had previously tried traditional networking groups but felt really awkward with the fake small talk that is inevitable in such marketing groups. I also didn't see the networking groups translate into actual business revenues so it felt fruitless to spend what precious marketing time I had on ventures that didn't produce any real results.

The Beginning of Our Special Group

Not too many days later after the Dude-Holy-Roller luncheon, I went over to Wendy's office to mooch some notary skills from her and I mentioned that I had visited that group. At the time, Wendy and I rented office space in the same executive-office complex. She humored me once in a while by allowing me to get documents notarized.

We talked about what I liked about the other organization and what I didn't. I mentioned that I really wanted to find a network of women business owners. We agreed that we knew of industry-specific groups that met. Those groups seemed problematic in being free to really share company secrets, if you will, because you have your local competitors sitting right next to you.

Wendy said she would ask around about groups that were open for women business owners. I took my newly notarized paperwork and off to "therapize" I went. I didn't think again about that conversation with Wendy. That is, not until we ran into each other in the halls of the office building—and guess what?

That crazy woman went and formed a group of women

business owners. Wendy said that she had found a great facilitator named Lauren Midgley and that other women were being invited.

She said that we (did you catch the "we"?) were going to meet in our conference room. That room that is right next door to my office? That room that would be really awkward for me to walk by if I didn't attend this meeting? This meeting that was theoretically part of my idea and all of Wendy's follow-through?

Oh damn.

Now I was going to have to attend. No getting out of this one. No blaming the manliness, overly zealous religiousness, or expensive entry fee. I just hoped this new group of women business owners didn't completely suck and wasn't an utter waste of the little off time I had in my schedule.

In the beginning, I had no real concrete expectations of the new mastermind group. Aside from the other organizations previously mentioned, I had nothing to compare it to so I was naïve of what it could be or what it might not be.

Initially, I honestly didn't spend much time thinking about the formation of the group. I was busy running my business and keeping my head above water. I knew we had a meet and greet scheduled and once it was on my calendar, I didn't think about it again.

I was aware that I had to at least look like I was taking it seriously and being a willing participant. I owed

Wendy that much. I had brought up wanting a group of women to meet with and she had made that happen.

I had to walk it out and see what was going to be created before I formally introduced why I might not be able to attend—even with them meeting on the other side of a wall of my office. I thought that I would wait until I submitted my "departure papers." You know, timing is everything.

At one point I thought I wouldn't have to draw up my exit papers because I was going to be weeded out. The other mastermind women liked the idea of meeting at some awful hour like 7:00 a.m. I wasn't entirely rejecting the early meeting because I think that is a cruel time but mostly because I am a mom. My child was in elementary school at the time and the earliest drop-off was 7:30 a.m.

I couldn't be in two places at once. As had happened other times in my career, motherhood was colliding with my owning a business. This time though, I wasn't too unhappy and thought maybe it was my natural out of the newly formed group.

If these women were going to be meeting on the other side of a wall of my office at 7:00 a.m., then I wouldn't have to slink by and not join them because I wouldn't be arriving to the office to see my first client until at least 10:00 a.m. and sometimes 11:00 a.m.

We would totally miss each other so I no longer had to feel guilty for not participating. As it turns out, the other ladies were agreeable to have our meetings begin at 8:00 a.m. I had previously said I could attend that time slot, so

Excuse #1 to escape the group quickly evaporated.

Even though I had previously told Wendy I wanted to join a business group, I was nervous about actually joining a group. Wanting and doing can be two entirely different things sometimes.

My Wing Women

On the day of our first face-to-face meeting, I arrived four minutes late (or close to it) because we were having our entire house flooring redone. My life was in a shambles that particular day. Construction people who had said they would arrive at a certain time decided that thirty minutes late was acceptable. It wasn't conducive to my schedule.

When they finally did arrive, out the door I flew to the meet and greet to be introduced to the other women who had expressed some interest in the mastermind group. My arrival a few minutes late was met by everyone else being present and already talking specifics about the group.

Whew. These women were not kidding around. As I took my seat, I realized that it had been a long time since I sat across from a group of women who were all so beautiful, put together, down-to-earth, and officially kick-ass smart.

It was immediately apparent that this was going to be an amazing synergy of women doing business life together. I was secretly doing happy somersaults on the inside.

Maybe I had found my wing women? I don't recall all the specifics of that meet and greet but I knew I was not going anywhere and my departure papers would not be drawn up.

This was exactly what I had been looking for and I knew it immediately. At that point, I didn't know what structure our group would take or how exactly we would function with one another. However, I knew there was a chemistry and dynamic nature of us being in the same room together. I immediately respected these women and their positions in the marketplace. I was very excited to get to know them better.

End of the Honeymoon

After the very first meeting for the meet and greet, I continued to enjoy the group dynamic and as we met regularly, our connection as women began to gel even deeper. A rich authenticity came to us as a mastermind group. However, as with everything, there is a phase of getting to know people that can be a little bit of a letdown.

For me, I had to overcome some challenges when the group was speaking directly about the business branding that I had created. At the onset of us meeting, I had been struggling with identifying with the Christian part of my business and branding for some time.

I had gone through a season in my own faith where I was having a hard time identifying with the local Southern church. I was really turned off to the Christianese that surrounded me within the culture, so when the mastermind group began speaking to me about my obvious hesitations about my business name (Southlake Christian Counseling), I had to really watch my frustration levels.

My faith and my business are so personal and I wasn't accustomed to having people poking around in either subject. I remember one meeting where Lauren made a direct suggestion. I recall cutting her off mid-sentence and telling her I wasn't going to do what she was talking about.

She, as always, was exceptionally gracious and adjusted herself to my obvious annoyance and, frankly, rudeness. I finished out that particular meeting by remaining fairly quiet. After the meeting ended, I recall sitting alone in my office doubting myself and my place in the group.

I had come to really value each of these amazing women and I didn't want to cut myself off from their insightful input but being transparent and then receiving honest feedback was really out of my comfort zone.

Ironic for the therapist, right?

I ask my clients to be willing to be open to new ways of thinking and behaving, but it was very hard for me initially to do that with the mastermind women. I made a decision right then: I would listen more when the mastermind women shared their ideas of how to positively impact my business.

I realized that I didn't have to implement every idea and that set me free from becoming internally defensive during our meetings. It really sunk into my spirit that I needed to allow myself to be a part of this group. Putting up my usual walls was going to set me on the outside of the bubble.

The magic was happening inside the group and that's where I needed to remain. I was one of the members of our group and they were a part of me. Why would I retreat from such positive connectedness? These were safe women. Women who truly cared about me and the success not only of my business but of me, as a friend.

It would have been tragic to walk away from that just because at the time I was very uncomfortable.

The Mojo, Magic, Synergy, and Energy

As I sit trying to figure out why our mastermind group has so greatly impacted me and my business life, I find myself at a loss of adequate words to convey the mojo, magic, synergy, and energy that is experienced when the five of us masterminds get together.

We just click.

As each of us arrives to our meetings, the energy in the room picks up and our individual pieces of the jigsaw puzzle start to fit together. Once all the members are present, we are a whole picture. We are one unit ready to take an honest and wise look at each of ourselves, our businesses, and each other.

I truly adore and admire each woman in the group. We may not all socialize with each other outside of our regularly held meetings but we are friends. We stay in touch, usually by text or email, throughout the weeks in between our meeting times.

When something great or something really crappy has happened in my business, these ladies are on the short list of whom I go to first with the important news. I know they authentically give a damn about me and the health of my business. I feel the exact same way about them. That bonds us all together. They are the ones I think to call or email when something BIG is happening with the business. I know their responses will be quick and heartfelt.

There is a genuine humor that our group shares. We have yet to leave a meeting without at least one good loud group laugh about something stupid or silly that one of us either thought or actually did.

We are messy humans and we have a special place to come and, as Lauren often says "open the kimono" and let it all hang out. Scary, I know. But honestly, it's so fabulous to have this level of transparency with good, healthy women.

We are messy humans and we have a special place to come and, as Lauren often says, "open the kimono" and let it all hang out. Scary, I know. But honestly, it's so fabulous to have this level of transparency with good, healthy women. We all need a place to come off the business stage and just be a person. Our mastermind group allows for each of us to do just that and I wish the same for you.

Going Forward

Being a part of the mastermind group has impacted my mind-set about my business in incredible ways. The structure of having a closed group of really dynamic women to share the business side of my life has created momentum in my business and myself as an entrepreneur.

I am no longer just wrestling within my own mind about how and where to take the business next in my master plan. The mastermind group allows me to have a confidential and supportive forum to bounce ideas around and dream about where I want myself and the business to go next.

It also is a wonderful bubble in which to share the hard side of business life and always be met with encouragement and wonderful ideas to consider. It is great to have these women to learn from—and to be able to celebrate with them the exciting things that are happening surrounding my business and theirs as well.

Staying committed to the mastermind group isn't hard at all for me. I can't even imagine going back to business life without this core group of wonderful women walking alongside me.

We had originally made a six-month commitment to the group and when the end of that time approached, I remember being incredibly worried and internally anxious that the other members might want to dissipate and I would be left without such a vital business-support system.

Happily, and a little to my surprise, the women each wanted to continue and expressed seeing as much value to our group as I felt. It really blessed me a lot to know that they wanted to continue doing business life together as much as I did.

That was a significant moment for me within the group. I wasn't the only one feeling the bond that had been created and it made me feel like I had a specific place within the group.

We are all different and from a variety of industries but there is a commonality among us that is hard to put into words. I think if I had to pin down the magic, it is that we all want to go for the top ring in life and are willing to take a positive, hopeful approach to reaching our life goals.

We are five women who are passionate about our industries, personal growth, and cheering one another on. Becoming a part of our mastermind group has truly been life changing for me.

I laugh as I think about the beginning and how much I tried to avoid joining the group. Sometimes we don't even know what's in our best interest.

I am glad life is sometimes so much smarter than I am.

Biography of Shannon Thomas

I **really, truly,** authentically understand the need to be an "overcomer" in life. Life has thrown some interesting twists and turns along my path. I strongly believe in the power of living to our fullest potential. We must have the ability to pull up our big-girl (or big-boy) panties and keep moving forward.

In a nutshell, I have had to become almost an entirely different person since my teens and twenties.

It includes overcoming debilitating panic attacks to go on to become a licensed therapist who mentors younger therapists.

It also includes dropping out of high school; eventually earning my master's degree at the age of thirty-four.

It also includes losing over 120 pounds.

No matter where we might find ourselves in life, we can make slow, steady changes that will add up and get us pointed in a new, healthier direction in life.

As the owner and lead therapist of Southlake Christian Counseling (SCC), it is my greatest desire that people find a place where they can feel comfortable to talk about anything and everything that is going on in their lives. It is very easy to hide our real feelings, even from those closest to us.

I began working with families in 2000, started in private practice counseling in 2007, and opened SCC in 2009. I have a bachelor's degree in legal studies from the University of California, Santa Cruz. I received my master of social work degree from San Jose State University. I am a Licensed Clinical Social Worker and Supervisor for postgraduate interns working toward their LCSW licensure. I am also a field instructor within the Master of Social Work program at Texas Christian University (TCU).

I am married with one son and have two very spoiled dog-children. I believe a key to finding lasting happiness in life is finding balance in our daily schedules to include: meaningful work, spiritual growth, regular exercise, authentic friendships, romantic love, attachment parenting, and hobbies.

"

Opportunity is missed by people because it is dressed in overalls and looks like work.

"

—Thomas Edison

Getting Your Mastermind Started

To get your mastermind group started, you will want to start with a vision of what you want it to be. You may model it after ones you have been part of in the past or ones that are in formation now.

To get your creative juices flowing, begin by using the simple **Who, What, Where, When, and Why** process. The standard five W's will work well to begin your thinking about how to create a mastermind that will serve you and your other members.

Who?

The people in your group are crucial to its success. If you have individuals who are all fully committed, then you might well be thrilled with the results. Invite people to your initial meet-and-greet session to share with them the vision you have for the mastermind group. Some may decide to stay and others may not. That is perfectly okay. Those who will see the vision and get excited are exactly the **Who** you want in your group.

You have a variety of options when creating the composition of the group. Here are some examples and ultimately some decisions to make as you craft your own mastermind group:

Local vs Virtual: There are many pros and cons to having a local group that meets in person or one that is made of up members who will connect virtually.

Industry or Profession Specific: Some mastermind groups are comprised of individuals who are involved in the same industry (real estate agents who work in different communities, for example) or who serve the same clients (attorney, counselor, nonprofit who serve the elderly, for example) or who are in completely different industries (health care, business, ministry, and so on) or any combination of the above. You get to decide. We chose our group to be comprised of professional business owners or self-employed service providers to expand our minds and bring multiple talents to the table.

Length of time in position or owning business: You may find it helpful for your group to be all at the same level of development in their business, or you may decide that having a variety of experience is helpful in expanding perspectives. Each member in our group is well beyond the start-up phase of her business. Each of our members is in high-growth mode in her business.

The important point on the **Who** is that the group must gel and be productive together. The variety of minds with varying points of view adds value to the group.

The individual personalities certainly have an impact on the group. You want to be certain that you are each better off in business because of each other. Using the DiSC or a similar personality-profiling tool, you may want to have your prospects share their profiles with each other.

For example, if you have all Dominants (which is the "D" of DiSC) in the mastermind group, you will need a strong set of ground rules, an understanding of expectations of each participant, and an ongoing evaluation of the value of the mastermind to its members.

If you have all Influencers (which is the "I" of DiSC) in the group, it might be hard to stay on track and get anything of substance done.

Ideally, a mix of all personalities—DiSC—likely will be a better blend—of sharing, input, points of view, and ways of thinking—that will lead to results.

Another angle to consider is understanding the StrengthsFinder characteristics of the prospects and ultimately of the members. Understanding each other's strengths will allow the group to tap into those strengths and magnify them.

It is important to pause for a moment and say that our mastermind group did not do any pretesting or personality screening prior to coming together. Although some of you may decide that personality screening is a good idea, others of you will not pursue this avenue. Just know that it has worked out wonderfully for us to allow the group to form with initially unknown strengths within the group.

We believe that our mastermind group has gelled well due to our deep mutual respect for one another. No one member in the group is trying to overpower the other members.

Thank goodness!

This is due in large part to Lauren's skillful leadership keeping us on track and in sync. Our group's personality dynamics work.

We are thankful for that gift.

Last, a key component of a successful mastermind group is the members' ability to trust each other to the highest degree. There will be confidential information shared. As such, you may even have members sign a confidentiality agreement. Regardless of the formality level you choose, seek individuals with high values and high principles.

This last point is a fundamental core principle of successful mastermind groups. If you compromise on this, then you will spend time on creating the mastermind group and you will be disappointed in the results. When problems occur (and they will), you will be able to point to flaws in a member's values and principles.

The deeper **Who** questions—keep in mind which model (composition of the group) will produce the best results:

1. Who in your network might be interested?
2. Who in your network's network might be interested?
3. Who is ready at this time and committed to take action?

What?

The **What** you are seeking to accomplish with the master-mind group and how will this happen. Think of this area of your mastermind group as the process, policies, and procedures.

Each mastermind group is different based on its unique participants and mission.

Major components to consider:
- Recruiting and selecting members
- Defining what's expected of the members, such as preparation, attendance, commitments, contributions
- Creating the meeting schedule, theme of each meeting
- Facilitating the meetings
- Documenting the meetings with audio recording or notes

Our group had loose guidelines on the above areas. Keeping in mind your group and need for control, you will want to think through what is most important. For example, our members were asked to be committed and show up prepared for the first six months.

If after six months they no longer wanted to be part of the group, then that would have been the appropriate time to leave the group. We believed that a full six months was needed for someone to evaluate the impact of the mastermind group for them personally and professionally.

The deeper **What** questions:
1. What are the policies of your mastermind group?
2. What is the enforcement process? Who is the enforcer?

3. What happens if a member is not following the rules?
4. What are the major topics this group will be discussing, (business development, leadership, productivity, customer service, personal development)?

Where?

The **Where** is an important factor. The big decision involves finding a suitable location for meeting that allows a confidential environment. You will want a working space with tables, whiteboards, room to spread out, and possibly a wall screen to project a PowerPoint presentation.

Select a centralized location that will make it easy for members to attend the meetings. A consistent location is important, rather than moving around for each meeting. From the beginning, our group utilized the conference rooms of various members' offices. We have also met at different member's homes when we were going to be meeting for longer periods of time.

The deeper **Where** questions:

1. What facilities are available during the times you want to meet?
2. Will it be free or low cost? If there is a cost, how will it be paid? Will there be dues to pay such expenses?
3. Is the location easy to access and park at?
4. Does this facility provide the needed amenities to conduct effective meetings?

When?

The **When** is the frequency of the meetings that will allow for maximum connection among the members. Frequency will vary among mastermind groups based on the needs.

Adding in a virtual component (phone or email or Skype) allows you to increase the frequency as needed.

Our group meets twice each month. We have selected the first and third Thursdays of each month. Doing so allows the members to count on a consistent meeting that can be put into the calendar. Having a set schedule and time allows for easy future calendaring.

Occasionally, we shift the date if one or more members are unable to meet on that date. We try not to schedule a time to meet unless all five of us can be present. Our deep respect for one another and the value that each member brings makes it an easy decision to navigate busy schedules in order to have all five members present.

> *Occasionally, we shift the date if one or more members are unable to meet on that date. We try not to schedule a time to meet unless all five of us can be present.*

There have been times when we were able to meet only one time per month. When that has occurred, we all have felt somewhat out of sorts. At the next meeting, it seemed like we had pent-up information and needed to expand the time for that one meeting to catch up about our businesses.

Consistency is the key.

In today's busy world, it can be a challenge to find a time that works for everyone. It is likely that individuals will need to evaluate and weigh the options of what they had previously scheduled and the benefits of the mastermind group.

For our group, each woman has made attending our meetings a high calendar priority. We can count on one hand the number of times that a member had to cancel at the last minute or couldn't come to a scheduled meeting. The five of us just make it happen.

We almost never miss our mastermind meetings.

Period.

It would be far too easy to let phone calls, texts, emails, staff issues, business meetings, or other distractions get in the way. One of the critical components of our group is that we show up on time and are mentally present. Phones are left in our purses or briefcases during our meetings. We let the outside world take care of itself during the hour and a half.

Thus, we are a much stronger, more connected mastermind group as a result.

The deeper **When** questions:

1. How often will the members need to meet to serve the interest of the members and the group?
2. What flexibility is needed to still meet and keep the group on track?
3. How often will you evaluate the effectiveness of the meeting schedule, such as every three or six months?

4. Will you have regular meetings during the month but also include longer retreats?

Why?

Why is a critical question to ask as you begin this journey.
- Why do you want to be part of a mastermind group?
- Why do you think it will help your business's success?
- Why do you think you can help others' businesses be successful?

Many of you may have heard of mastermind groups. There will be others who are just now learning about the power of a mastermind group. Have you already heard of the successes others have had with their mastermind group? Maybe you have thought about this topic for a while. Have you heard of others' successes, maybe felt a bit jealous, wanted to join theirs…and then, the thought hits you…I should just start my own!

If so, **YOU** are the catalyst for making your mastermind group happen. Your **Why** must be big enough to sustain the masterminding of the mastermind.

The play on words is deliberate.

If you go into creating the mastermind group in a half-assed way, then the results you will achieve will be the same: half-assed. The group will need an informal leader who pays attention to the details, such as consistent schedule, location, theme for each meeting, member recruitment, and most important, oversight of members' needs being met.

We honor that you are reading this book to figure it out

and do it right, whatever "right" way you determine is yours.

Your answers to the questions below will create your road map. We suggest you begin writing answers to these questions, either on paper or electronically. By doing so, you will organize and refine your thoughts with each iteration.

So, the deeper **Why** questions:

1. Why is participating in a mastermind group important to YOU at this time?
2. What is the Why of this group?
3. Why would someone want to join this group?
4. Why would this group want to select that person? Consider that person's strengths.
5. Why might their business fit well with the others in the group?

As you can see, there are many questions and answers to consider as you create the mastermind group that will work for you. If possible, find a partner who is interested to help you.

"

The elevator to success is out of order. You'll have to use the stairs... one step at a time.

"

—Joe Girard

Action Items for You to Get Started

Once you have planned the concept of your mastermind, it is time to get started.

1) Establish the facilitator:

Work first on your facilitator. Whether that will be you or a "Lauren" you know—begin there. Brainstorm and list your remaining ideal **Whos**; the ideal members to recruit. Your facilitator, however, is going to be crucial on day one, so solidify that relationship first.

*2) Invite your remaining **Whos** to an introductory meeting:*

Set a time and place for the introductory meeting. The date and time should be a firm one. As the group is formed, other decisions such as the future schedule may be set democratically.

However, your first meeting is a crucial one. It will serve to establish the priority level of potential members and prevent the introductory meeting from being perpetually rescheduled. By remaining firm about the first meeting's time and place, you will find out who is truly interested and potentially committed.

At this point, you have thought through your goals and vision for your group. Next, it is time to send out the invitations. Give the potential members a clear idea of your vision and how and why you believe they would be a valuable member. Be prepared for follow-up inquiries. Consider in advance how you might address questions and concerns.

Key considerations include:

- What if the person cannot make it to the first meeting?
- Would it be satisfactory to accept their commitment and welcome them to join on meeting two?
- What if they have a friend or business acquaintance that they want to invite?
- Are you agreeable to opening the group to others?
- Do you feel safer controlling the membership, limiting it to people you personally know?

Determining your answers to these questions in advance and sticking to a preset policy will make the initial meeting run more smoothly. The more clarity you have to share with potential group members, the stronger mastermind group you are creating.

3) Set an agenda and rules:

Once you have a general mission in place, communicate this to the potential members in your initial communication. Before the first meeting, finalize an agenda with a general plan or outline for future meetings.

Draft a mission statement for the group. Determine the level of formality you want for the group policies. If you have a small and local group, then you may be perfectly comfortable getting everyone's verbal agreement to the group rules.

However, as you consider larger numbers or a broader geographic area, you might consider a written agreement—including nondisclosure or confidentiality agreements. For example, you could have a group agreement with absentee policies. You may want to set in place a firm policy for removal of a member who is unproductive or is distracting to the group dynamic.

Setting out clearly defined policies and expectations such as meeting attendance, confidentiality, preparedness, and participation will minimize frustration and conflict later.

4) Structure your meetings:

Determine the frequency, location, and time of the meetings. At this point, you may decide to have this process be more democratic in order to arrive at a schedule that meets the needs of the members. Be cognizant of the location, however. A local coffeehouse or restaurant may not be the ideal choice for regular meetings. The members need to be able to share in confidence, so ideally choose a private location with minimal risk of interruptions.

The group facilitator might assist you in or take charge of setting a structure and topics for the regular meetings. It is extremely important to have an agenda for the first meeting, because that will set the tone for future meetings.

Think through possible structures and choose one for the regular meetings. Here are some ideas of possible meeting structures:

1) Every member is allotted time to present or speak at

every meeting. They will spend a portion of their allotted time discussing how the topic affects their business, and the remaining time will be open for group input, advice, and ideas. For example, if our group of five members is meeting for ninety minutes, each person has fifteen minutes.

2) For larger groups, a single topic might be discussed for multiple meetings, so that the members have ample time to provide their perspective and ask questions of the group.

3) You could consider a format where two members speak during a specific meeting, thus allowing for longer time to fully discuss their business.

4) Determine a specific frequency (such as once a quarter), when a single member may dominate the full time slot with a particular topic. The other members may advise, give input, or have a shorter time to discuss how the key speaker's topic relates to them and their own business.

5) Guest speakers may be brought in for a portion of the meeting time. The group can discuss how the topic presented applies to their business.

Of course, it is your mastermind, so you may structure it in any way you wish. However, we advise you to make it a priority that each member has equal and ample opportunity to share and receive input from the group.

Some of our mastermind meeting topics:

• What is your biggest challenge in the next thirty days

in your business?

- Provide the group a ninety-day progress report: accomplishments, key decisions made, key people connections, stickiest situation encountered, and then two or three action items for the next ninety days.
- What is your most pressing decision to make right now and why is it so important?
- What is your overall client-strategy plan? The plan should encompass new growth, VIP clients, attraction, retention, acquisition costs, and new markets to pursue.
- How visible are you in your marketplace? How could you "amp it up"?
- Name key successes in past ninety days.
- What are your productivity secrets?
- How do you track your key performance indicators in your business?
- Present an existing situation you need feedback on.
- Create a brainstorming session on something completely new that would significantly impact your business.
- What is the one thing that you need to get done in your business?"
- What are your goals for the upcoming year? Declare them.
- What are your top three successful marketing strategies?

We have explained the details that will help get you started. You will be amazed how beneficial your Mastermind can be—with the right group, the right mindset and the right topics.

"

The difference between
successful people and very
successful people
is that very successful
people say no
to almost everything.

"

—Warren Buffet

Conclusion

Our purpose in writing this book is to share with you how we created a successful mastermind group, where each member looks forward to attending the meeting.

We wanted you to get to know us through our stories and perspectives. It is our hope that you will be inspired to create your own mastermind group.

Ours has been extremely beneficial to the five of us. We believe there is a bit of magic that makes this group so valuable. We know that you can create a successful group, too.

A productive and successful group can be established many different ways. Give yourself the freedom to think outside of previously held ideas of what a business group can be.

Our group was created for women in business and the members are from different industries. It is highly likely that a vibrant group could be formed that is co-ed, has members from related businesses, or is a group of employees. The number of configurations is endless.

How will you bring your mastermind group to fruition?

First, have the desire for it, and then go make it happen within your own circle of community. Do you know someone who might be a great facilitator like our Lauren?

Do you know someone who is a connector and can help bring everyone together similar to the way our Wendy did for us?

Do you know a "Nicole" who doesn't want yet another traditional networking group but rather an informal board of directors?

Do you know a "Shannon" who knows that something is missing in his or her business life but has not found the right piece yet?

Maybe you are or know a "Sarah" who has experienced rapid growth in business and needs a safe place to be authentic and to confidentially discuss challenges she faces.

It doesn't matter which one of us five masterminds you find yourself relating to the most. We each have our unique voice and perspective that adds to the collective magic of our mastermind group.

Take a few moments and think about one person in your network that you know and admire. Think what it would be like to include them in your mastermind. Reach out to them and explore their interest.

Right now.

Go do it. Pick up the phone, walk down the hall, or send an email. Do whatever makes the most sense and begin the initial contact to share your ideas of a new group.

As you use the tools outlined in the previous chapters, you use a tested road map to be able to re-create what we have experienced.

We, the five masterminds, promise you that it will be time well spent. You will be wisely investing in the power to radically transform you and your business life.

We wish you all the best in creating the ideal-for-you mastermind group.

Please share your stories with us. We want to hear about your success and those who are in *your* mastermind group.

RESOURCES

Contact Information

If you are interested to know more about the mastermind processes, information presented in this book or book us to speak, please contact us.

Powerof5Minds Partnership

www.Powerof5Minds.com
questions@Powerof5Minds.com

Join us on Facebook:
Follow us on Twitter: @Powerof5Minds
Connect with us on LinkedIn: **Linked** .

Sarah Gilliland
G & G Law Firm
www.southlakelaw.com

Wendy Knutson
Knutson CPA
www.KnutsonCPA.com

Lauren Midgley
Courage to Succeed Consulting
www.LaurenMidgley.com

Nicole Smith
Briggs Freeman | Sotheby's Intl. Realty
www.NicoleSmith.net

Shannon Thomas
Southlake Christian Counseling
www.southlakecounseling.org